New Transgender Blockbusters

New Transgender Blockbusters

Oscar Upperton

Victoria University of Wellington Press

Victoria University of Wellington Press
PO Box 600, Wellington
New Zealand
vup.wgtn.ac.nz

A catalogue record is available at the National Library of New Zealand

ISBN 9781776562992

Published with the assistance of a grant from

ARTS COUNCIL OF NEW ZEALAND *TOI AOTEAROA*

Printed by Markono Print Media, Singapore

Contents

Atlas

Last year's trees are dropping.
They drop like sticky fruit.
They drop as the flies rise.
Last year I woke up differently.
This year is the same old mess.

The dead see different centuries
like I see fruit on a tree,
like I see land from the sea.
The ocean climbs the mast.
The years pass. They pass.

I want to go to Atlas, which is not Atlantis.
I want to give this continent a map.
There is never not something
that doubles back. I am inverting.
I am inventing a new way to act.

Dark night

Dark night. Full of drums.
Wait in the line for friends.
This is the before picture,
before the world ends.
Blue screen. Yellow butter.
Film rattles round the bend.
Want to run. But can't run.
Shut your eyes. Pretend.

Door against the cold
for Mum

Someone is dying tonight.
Someone always is. A life springs up,

then folds together. White rocks,
a last drink, a black umbrella.

Mum brings in wood, two under each arm.
She could have carried us like that.

Across the street, in moonlight,
she squints at something.

The dead should come back changed,
or what's the point? The beach cools,

she hums. Hand over hand,
the stacks of kindling.

The waves flicker, the harbour's brewing.
The ship is a sort of dark undoing.

Yellow house

We're eels in the grass. The nights are ours,
blue nights beckoning. The lambs are jolly
in their steel float.

The yellow house yellows. Old books sit
and swing their feet. Might be neat to know
what they're talking.

The stream crosses the bridge. Pūkeko flicker
from blue to white. Bikes rust into each other.
We rust at table.

The black dog walks to the end of the hills.
The cat walks herself. The stream burns.
We look and look at it.

Explaining yellow house

Eels as in steals. The grass as in our element.
Lambs as in their prams. Float as in hover
above the world in boxes.

Yellow as in olden times. Books as in wait
in the hot car. As in talk mischief, as in sit
in a tree with a book.

Stream as in steam. Pūkeko as in flickering light.
Rust as in iron oxidising, as in fire, as in table
compromised.

Dog as in Chuckie. Cat as in Fizz. Look
and look as in Pip Adam, *The New Animals*,
page 147, line 10.

Song about a child

The dog is a book read over and over
The dog is a river that's stopping for no one
The dog is a child who thinks hot is a colour

The book is a dog that's waiting for water
The book is a river that cannot be forded
The book is a child who's made out of silence

The river is a dog running past hillsides
The river is books spilt down a staircase
The river is a child who won't do the dishes

The child is a dog sniffing at thistles
The child is a book that hasn't been written
The child is a river running under a river

The child is the dog and the dog is the river
The book is a book about children in winter
The dog barks a book at the edge of the river
Dog sings the child sings it over and over

Child's First Dictionary

for Tess

White flowers and red berries
means ghost notes in the attic.

A chicken in a cat cage
means horribly rising static.

New lambs buried in the garden
means love has come to stay.

Passionfruit cut on the vine
means trim the old bouquet.

Witchy foxglove fingers
means history has touched you.

Cats asleep on bunk beds
means turn the earth anew.

My pine-tree house, your pine-tree house,
means disturbed summer rest.

Rabbit bones under the pig house
means the autumn trees are blessed.

The nail caught in your knee that day
means things are not as I remember.
For me it was September.
For you it was December.

Numbers

One is holy.
Two is me and Tess.
Three is holy.
Four is me and Tess and Ben and Tan.
Five is a full car.
Six is the family number.
Seven is not lucky.
Eight is not counting thumbs.
Nine is the planet number.
Ten I don't think about.

Manawatū

Stones in my pocket. Slingshot in my hand.
Lambs trying to stand. Sally Army band.

Fence without neighbours. Stage without script.
Enter left, leave right. Two by two. Don't trip.

The riverside purple. The hall gone white.
The sky's going gold. Come along inside.

It's all right. It's more than all right.
The people light. The hilltops light.

Growing upside down

The dog gets in his last licks.
Pollen blows in from the long paddocks.
The chair rocks itself. The door unlatches.
The sun detaches. The evening watches.
Insects waver in the breeze,
read the weather from their crowded tree.
The brothers give the cat a tease.
Dad's plugged in to overseas.
Uruguay Panama. Crimea Canada.
Belarus India. New Hampshire Canberra.
The map's upside down. What's the right way to fall?
The planet turns. We have a ball.

Dutch instruction

for Henk and Cilia

Optimism is the idea that it not always will rain.
Leave home as soon as you are free,
for everyone comes back again—

just never board a train
without a member of family.
Optimism is the idea that it not always will rain,

that between sea and plain
will always sprout a city.
For everyone comes back again.

Do not treat land reclaimed
as you would the earth itself. Usually,
optimism is the idea that it not always will rain,

but sometimes it is a plane
in a white sky.
For everyone comes back again,

they return aboard their vessels of love. That is in translation
(from the Māori, a song). See,
optimism is the idea that it not always will rain
for everyone. Come back again.

Recipe book
from the Katherine Mansfield House

American soup. Half turnip.
Linseed liquorice and chloroform lozenge.
1500 new economy dishes.
One carrot. One onion. Neck of mutton.
The spaces at the end of each chapter
may be used with advantage for entering personal recipes.

Garden beds

My years are planted back there
somewhere. The garden gathers
rain. The garden pulls the things
it needs from air. Mutters to me
years were better before the rain.

Door-ajar rain.
Picture-perfect
window pane.

Years aren't to blame. I was always old.
The garden gathers rain. I grew and grew
and broke the mould. I sat there in the rain.

The bus

The bus wanted to travel.
He saw the same town every day
but when he was swung around the corners in the morning
(facing north)
he saw mountains.
What it would be like to drive up a mountain.
He would drive up the side of it
and feel the snow crunch under his wheels.
He imagined that snow would creak under him
like the floor of the old Kilbirnie warehouse. It would protest
at his weight on its back. The snow would want to be other places,
the floor other places still.

Dark night

Dark night. Doldrums.
Waiting for friends.
This is the before picture
so shut your eyes. Pretend.
Want to run. But can't run.
Film rattles round the bend.

Second home

The second home is always in the shadow of the first.
We are far from music. We listen to the birds.
We are far from chocolate. We fast.
We are far from safe harbours. We dig and dig.

There was once a dance in a vegetable garden,
a boat as a present, a smooth upshoot of bubbles in a glass.
There was a way of saying that was like giving.
We do not talk this way now.

We are not committing to this horizon.
The ocean will sedately swallow us.
We cannot live in the light of these stars.
We are but weathering a tempest here.

New transgender blockbusters

If we put on make-up the camera won't linger
and we'll change our clothes out of frame
or if we change our clothes in frame it will be done casually,
talking as we shrug T-shirts over our heads
or pulling on the spacesuit to try to fix the loose coupling
one last time. We won't die, or if we die,
we'll die surrounded by our grandchildren, handing out bequests
of stolen property and vowing vengeance on rival families.
We'll travel in time, and save the world,
and doom the world but not in an earthquake-causing,
crime-against-nature sort of way.
We'll have transgender friends and family members,
the frame of the film sustaining with ease the image
of transgender people talking to each other.
We'll all be very very brave
because being a person requires great bravery,
and we won't have to wear signs around our necks saying
I am a Person.
We'll become immune to all tropes, and win every prize.
If we find a gun under the floorboards in the first act,
we will bring world peace by the fourth act.
If we open our lockets to show the platoon
a photograph of our loved one,
we'll be guaranteed to survive until the end credits.

Oscar Wilde named himself after me

Doesn't everyone name themselves? See the old names come back in the baby name books: Noah, Oscar, Leo, Noah, Noah. How does everyone else cope without an awards ceremony named after them? Dad said Oscar is the name of someone who ran away and joined the circus. Toby too. I must find a Toby and we will run away together. Oscar: deer-lover, forest of deer. Norse spear. I ran away and joined it in the forest.

Wētā

Darkness forgets my eyes in moments.
Light will never need reminding.
I'm just pretending to be mad.
You know I'm clockwork. I need rewinding.

You shouldn't step on the gates of heaven
when I draw them in the sand.
The wētā was better when fixed on paper.
It looks so sad now in your hand.

Grief won't be the real disaster.
That hides in a more familiar place.
The wētā is another sound forgotten,
clicks unanswered out in space.

The answer room is through this door.
I will meet my answer here.
She will build me a quiet corner.
She will want to join me there.

Lonely crow

The river knows what the lonely crow did
when the others left in the noonday sun.
What crying happens under rapids,
what happens when the running's done?

What's with the bees that rise around us
like a city's elevators?
Why can't we all be cute and famous,
and set upon by demonstrators?

What could be hotter than a rocker
dancing in prescription glasses?
Why is the gardener so macabre
about his taxidermy classes?

Nothing sadder than a lonely river.
Nothing darker than a single crow.
Shiver at the strong's surrender.
Play a tune on your June piano.

Slice of life

The golden guards
are statues clapping.
The sound of the yard

is axes lopping.
We still swear by the castle air
for curing a trap that won't stop yapping.

The queen plucks a tissue.
She can't stop laughing.
Her black-coated issue

is plotting murder.
When she said *Grow up*
he bloody heard her.

This is why

he loosed the boat that sank the ship
he muttered swears and gave us lip

he took white sailboats from the girls
he swallowed whole the summer pearls

he took red berries from the boys
he gave the dead a waking voice

he shook the baby in the cot
he left the cabbages to rot

he spat into the casserole
he left the dreamer down the hole

he smashed the glass-spun hummingbird
he wouldn't use the magic word

he took our tongues and gave us lies
he made the graveman improvise

he slapped the spinster in the face
he broke the boy who won the race

he disembowelled our finest cow
he told us to start running now

he dyed the wedding dresses red
he filled the old man's head with lead

and this is why we want him dead
and this is why we want him dead

Small talk

How've you been have you
mastectomy or
called dyke at a bus stop

How do you find Wellington do you
trapped or
it will be taken from you

What do you do do you
produce or
your wound that no one talks about

What do you do outside of work do you
counselling or
keeping the baby alive

What's your favourite what's your
things on fire or
things yet to be on fire

Do you want kids do you want
girls or
kids

What kind of music do you like do you
birds screaming or
heterosexual wedding playlist

What do you do to relax do you
visit the grave or
childless

Am I terrified am I
are we all or
alone

Prudence

She slipped inside and tried a meow
like she had heard cats make in the city
food appeared
she was on to a good thing
she drank water from an old ice-cream container
she had her own food bowl on the stairs
she had a name
Prudence
the other sang it and made rhymes of it
even when she wasn't on the knee
or at the ankle
she had her own bedroom
that the other sometimes slept in
when winter came she sat on the knee
and watched the gas heater blue flame burn
she was replete with food and warmth
and she realised love
as she was scratched between her ears
and heard
now Pru
what shall we watch tonight
and she wondered
if she revealed herself
would she still be invited onto the knee when it was cold
would there still be food on the seventh stair
would she still be consulted

on what to watch each night
would she be allowed the blue flame
while the other watched *Seinfeld*
who could ever love her
but she was loved
she held these two thoughts in her head
it was starting to rain outside
Pru had an inside now
tree branches scraped against the window panes
Jerry made a joke about driving to the airport

Don't let that chair be the only chair

It doesn't like it. That towel,
fold it, put it away
with its fellows in the linen cupboard.
It is a cold night, bring in the hose,
let it coil underfoot,
let it listen to the radio.
Close the doors.
Let not the curtains part.
Insert both keys at once
so one isn't alone in the dark.

Apartments at 11pm

Work is great. It stops the thinking. The thinking comes later like a tide rising in the night, like the stars turning on. Look at it this way—it's a forest. And the trees are all good, and the grass is all good, but there's something wrong with the air. It's gone. And the trees don't sway, they twitch like a pack of horses in a storm. Twitching in the no-air. But it's all good. The trees are sickening with health. The flowers fat and the leaves so green. The grass thick underfoot. Water bubbling up. Where is it all coming from. And for how much longer.

It's that time again time to repress every social interaction scrub cleanse rinse so you can begin tomorrow anew tomorrow being Saturday so there's a chance to be good because you can stay home and look through the safe window the one you can't be seen from. Drown the anecdotes drown the advice. Don't think about your friends your hopes your body repress the sound of your voice and the shape your face makes when you breathe. Put today's jokes in a locked box place the box in the bottom of your wardrobe lock the wardrobe twice and burn the house down.

Cold night. Oil creaks in the heater. Falling deeper into bed. Voices in the dark above speak beautiful nonsense. Falling deeper. Perfect, perfect world. The window open. The curtain's shunt-shunt against the wind. Might they come tonight, the dead? My aunt, my mother, my brother. The older ones whose faces have been rubbed out. I'm dreaming. Sit up,

stare the dark out, listen. Hear the usual sound, the cat head-
butting the bedroom door. I let her in, us both unsmiling,
lift her onto the bed. She takes a turn about the duvet,
preens, settles. Comes to rest on my chest under my chin.

Today was a muffin day. Jodie at table acting like the cat that got
in the cream. Her paws were white. Muttering to herself like an
old woman. But you know what they say. It's the first sign. The
second's coming. She's out of the box. Like cats in boxes, one
is always out. You can't keep them still to get the picture. The
picture-perfect cub in the snow, tail in her mouth, keeping warm.
Even Christmas is cold now. A glove for each hand—everything
provided: ticket, hotdog, seat beside the ice rink. Incroyable,
ma petite. Every cloud has a silver surfer. Marvel. Marvellous!

Mount Victoria

Night's breath on the glass.
The last long blast of the ferry.
Cars stacked in the cul-de-sacs.
The cat watches everything
with a yellow eye. Pickpocketing between houses,
past enemies asleep in folding chairs,
I see students tucked abed
beneath their childhood drawings.
In the back of a car someone is drugged,
thought he was with friends.
Another takes the bus.
What else? Parsley grows in the gutters,
garlic blooms under the trees.
The cat's yellow eye regards.
Night herbs, day breaks, soft breath, glass.

Panic attack

Attack me. Attach to me. The blue sky is in the sky, pressing so blue. A glass plate covers the stone. Alone. What's ringing in the doorbell? Who heard the flight of stairs? Prepared to ring in the morn the mid the eve they all crowd senseless. This is a breathing exercise. Count the rivers. Breathe quicker. Manawatū Clutha. Waikato Pohangina. Sky drops to ground floor. Breathe closer. Glass plate sharp with uncracked face. Breathe closer. Sky against skin. Water louder. Smile. Air water. Throat clatter. Sky in mouth. Breathe closer.

This is a breathing exercise

Our hands are numb.
Start breathing.

Watch the plate on the stone.
It has been there a long time.

It is surrounded by air.
The trees rest against the air.

The plate is glass
and it sits on a grey stone.

The sky is blue
and blue sits in it.

The trees bring in their years
and let out sighs of oxygen.

Might we rest a while, rest in the trees,
in the leaves? Let the sky blue out and out,

let ourselves loosen, hold blue,
surround air. We are stone
and we sit on grey glass.

Allergy

He would sneeze at anything.
He was allergic to pollen,
contact with physical objects,
and animals that loved him.
He would swell up when he saw a plane—do you remember?
And his throat would close over if he heard the word 'elevator'.
Lift, please say lift, he'd choke
while fumbling for his EpiPen.
No need to be fancy around me.
Reading this aloud would have sent him six feet under—
if he hadn't had his EpiPen with him, which he always did.
He worked in a museum. He sneezed underground.
At night he would sneeze in bed, naked, no covers,
his body lumpy with hives. His cat, who loved him,
would dab at his tears with her small black paws.

Prayer

Snow falls around the hut.
Now fall the ground beneath me.
Glory oh glory. Glory to—

Mānuka. Snow under ferns.
Flax under siege.
The prince of death is come
and stalks the hills oh praise—

Smoke trudges out the chimney.
The dog whimpers, the fire rests.
Praise be to the light that burns,
the heat that shakes the world.
Its majesty, its majesty, raining—

All the creatures in the bush know it.
The sound that opens heads alive.
Split the dog's brain. Split
the fantail's brain. Split
the spider's brain. Split
the axe's brain—

Snow falls into our heads.
Steam in the mountains—

Caroline

In the beginning there was nothing.
There was nothing for a long long time.
I want to play in the sandpit, said Caroline.
Might I be allowed? Might I?
The Earth shrieked and coalesced.
It was her only birthday, but she'd had it before.
The same tectonics. Wanting to build in the sand
a park in which a queen could saunter.
So long to go. Oh Caroline, oh Caroline,
so many ages before sandpits.
The trees, the fish must have their age.
The dragonflies alighting on peaks like helicopters.
The earth will rise, the rocks will rise to greet you,
springing from peaks like mountain goats.

There was nothing for a long long time.
I want to play in the sandpit, said Caroline.
Might I be allowed? Might I?
The Earth shrieked and coalesced.
It was her only birthday, but she'd had it before.
The same tectonics. Wanting to build in the sand
from six to seven. But six is all. She is all
the world holds. The land is hers,
a park in which a queen could saunter.
So long to go. Oh Caroline, oh Caroline,
so many ages before sandpits.

The trees, the fish must have their age.
The dragonflies alighting on peaks like helicopters.
The earth will rise, the rocks will rise to greet you.

I want to play in the sandpit, said Caroline.
Might I be allowed? Might I?
The Earth shrieked and coalesced.
It was her only birthday, but she'd had it before.
The same tectonics. Wanting to build in the sand
from six to seven. But six is all. She is all
there is, cradling the last dinosaur in her arms,
its face ashy, hers like the setting sun. Endings are all
the world holds. The land is hers,
a park in which a queen could saunter.
So long to go. Oh Caroline, oh Caroline,
so many ages before sandpits.
The trees, the fish must have their age.
The dragonflies alighting on peaks like helicopters.

Might I be allowed? Might I?
The Earth shrieked and coalesced.
It was her only birthday, but she'd had it before.
The same tectonics. Wanting to build in the sand
from six to seven. But six is all. She is all
there is, cradling the last dinosaur in her arms,
trying to learn this new thing, pain.

She wants to be good. The Earth now silent,
its face ashy, hers like the setting sun. Endings are all
the world holds. The land is hers,
a park in which a queen could saunter.
So long to go. Oh Caroline, oh Caroline,
so many ages before sandpits.
The trees, the fish must have their age.

The Earth shrieked and coalesced.
It was her only birthday, but she'd had it before.
The same tectonics. Wanting to build in the sand
from six to seven. But six is all. She is all
there is, cradling the last dinosaur in her arms,
trying to learn this new thing, pain.
There isn't a way back, a way to stop this.
Eggs ripped open like birthday presents.
She wants to be good. The Earth now silent,
its face ashy, hers like the setting sun. Endings are all
the world holds. The land is hers,
a park in which a queen could saunter.
So long to go. Oh Caroline, oh Caroline,
so many ages before sandpits.

It was her only birthday, but she'd had it before.
The same tectonics. Wanting to build in the sand
from six to seven. But six is all. She is all

there is, cradling the last dinosaur in her arms,
trying to learn this new thing, pain.
There isn't a way back, a way to stop this.
She's an undertaker. A census-taker of extinction,
a cataloguer of bones, teeth, skins, forests,
eggs ripped open like birthday presents.
She wants to be good. The Earth now silent,
its face ashy, hers like the setting sun. Endings are all
the world holds. The land is hers,
a park in which a queen could saunter.
So long to go. Oh Caroline, oh Caroline.

Dark night

Dark night. Dark lights.
Drumming up friends.
Last night in the doldrums.
Shut your eyes. Pretend.

Home sick

I am sick for a city that doesn't exist.[1]
I hide in my room, on my dead-end road,
the lead-lined red box that shuts with a twist.[2]

Morning alarms rise up with the mist.[3]
The horses are yellow, their manes overgrown.
I am sick for a city that doesn't exist.[4]

Glowing watch faces on every wrist,[5]
and velvet at throats for the evening shows.
The lead-lined red box that shuts with a twist.[6]

My daughter pines with a limp and a lisp.[7]
She lies in a boat slung low with its load.
I am sick for a city that doesn't exist.[8]

1 The city was called Father, and Mother by other people.
2 Seal ourselves away, and all is forgiven.
3 Mist is water in air, and was free to use in younger times.
4 The city was called Father, and Mother by other people.
5 Numbers painted on by women with holes in their tongues.
6 Seal ourselves away, and all is forgiven.
7 Forests as far as we could see were taken.
8 The city was called Father, and Mother by other people.

In my room there's a table, on the table's a list.[9]
The names I locked up when I left on my own,
in the lead-lined red box that shuts with a twist.[10]

A key in my pocket, a key in my fist.[11]
Open and kill this world, let me go home.[12]
I am sick for a city that doesn't exist.[13]
The lead-lined red box that shuts with a twist.[14]

9   Order us according to how we were saved.
10   Seal ourselves away, and all is forgiven.
11   The answer room has locked its door.
12   Unlocking is a death played out in a keyhole.
13   The city was called Father, and Mother by other people.
14   Seal ourselves away and all might be forgiven.

Somebody to love

The crow found the human boy reading and raised him in a cage in the front garden. The frog found the human woman dancing and built her a dance studio with a heated floor. The fernbird drained the wetland and planted roses. The prize for best rose was a breeding pair. Oh, to win, to be a winner is a glorious thing because there can only be one.

Not even close. The fernbird pecked at her feet and cleared her throat. The frog took a picture of the woman climbing a tree. Get into the studio, he said, dance on the heated floor with your feet only and wag your tail-less butt. The spider ate Bear Grylls for the ratings. Business isn't a business, she said, it's a passion. The share market is a symphony orchestra. I conduct it so well, so finely.

The roses grew by the dance studio, along the road, into the front garden where the boy sat in his cage. He wrote warnings in his web in the darkest corner. Find me somebody to love. The song didn't mean anything to them but it meant something to him.

Poetry exercises

A poem with a hole in it.
A poem with a word missing.
A poem without nouns.
A poem with a torn map.
A poem with a hole inside it.
A poem with a hole at the bottom of the bag.
A poem with a word missing.
A poem with a hole in the heart.
A poem with an ending missing.
A poem that doesn't end.
A poem with a hole in its body.
A poem that has been machine-gunned.
A poem with a line of holes in its body.
A poem bleeding.
A poem with somebody missing.
A poem about a bus.
A villanelle whose footnotes form a sonnet.
A poem with nobody missing.

Carmen

She didn't know how not to be so when she left she lingered.
I don't know her. I shouldn't write about her.
This is a guess but when she talked
we went quiet.

I go quiet now.
The room is full of elders being still.
They watch me write and eat and grow older.
Must be nice, they say. *Do you know what we went through for you?*

She rests in Sydney, which is not her home. They cry about it,
the elders. I don't know her. I shouldn't cry.
She would have loved one dress
in particular.

I imagine her
laid out in it, beautiful, red, the crying
has gone on for years. She doesn't know me.
I want to cry for all of them. I can't. I shouldn't feel like this.

Cross-dresser

I am a pious woman.
I watch as the men leave for war.
I rake the garden over with my hands.
War visits on the roof of the church.
She sits like a great owl, hooting.
I turn my face away. I pray, Lord I pray.
A great evil is tramping over the face of my country.
An evil camps at the end of the river.
Evil has red hair and speaks harshly.
Evil wears helmets and carries pikes.
The Lord gives me a banner
and a cover of chainmail.
They are heavy and hurt my shoulders.
Men do not complain about this. They are weak;
they do not understand that which has been given to them so easily.
I hold a banner, which is a blasphemy.
I wear chainmail, which is a crime.
The Lord tells me I will burn for this and I cry in the garden.
I hide my face from Him in the dirt but He sees,
through the worms' eyes He sees me and He remembers
His son crying in a different garden to the east of here.
The Lord remembers His son crying,
and does not think, *How sad,* or
How cruel I was, or, *Such things are necessary*
but I wish I could have held him. The Lord simply remembers,
Yes, My son cried in a garden like this, the night I told him.

This was when the silver coins were paid and before the walk
to the place of crucifixion.
The Lord does not know that the walk felt longer than it was,
that spit fell on His son from the people shouting,
that oil had been spilt on the road and he had slipped and fallen
again and again. Each time a reminder that they did not love him.
He had been made to be loved, so this was painful to him.
I hold the banner before me. I do not bend, though it is heavy.
I walk with it held before me down the village lane.
I am a pious man. I was made strange, to a strange pattern.
Blue flowers nod me on my way. I will burn for this.

And the cattle are not orphans

And the picture was a present
And the shore had not been broken
And the cattle are not orphans

And the photo hadn't snapped yet
And I hadn't seen the body
And there wasn't time regardless

And the picture wasn't present
And the cattle trumped the living
And the silence well it's restful

And the pitcher wasn't breaking
And the living cows weren't moving
And the picture caught the paddocks

And the sun's come up real stellar
And the dark well it's a comfort
And the time regards us passing

And the crops how are they doing
And the most I'll miss is you love
And the pitching sea's a killer

And the midnight moonlight river
And the breaking call of cameras
And the picture snaps our colour
And there's not a breath among us

Lantern light

Cannon room. Soft delight.
Rattling fight. Mud platoon.
Fighting fit. Parlour's floor.
Blind allure. Iron bit.
Head device. Treasured caul.
Blank morale. Not advice.
Mighty fall. Good to go.
Aching slow. Dead appal.

Acre of snow. Dead applaud.
Nightly call. Goodbye go.
Back in old. Noted vice.
Head of lice. Threatened more.
Binding law. Lying wit.
Crying quick. Hole in wall.
Rat in flight. Bloody moon.
Crayon gloom. Lantern light.

Interrogation

Please talk to me. I'm a good listener. I won't correct your syntax
or try to change your mind or interrupt you.
Talk in the green-lined room on the fourth floor
or on the patio with an afternoon sun in the corner.
I'll listen. This building was built for listening.
My ears are in the walls. My ears
are in the food you're eating. I can play you tunes from Earth
if that would make you feel comfortable.
Eat my ears, talk to me, let me listen.
Don't touch the water that runs from the taps
at all hours. Let me do my job, of keeping you safe
and keeping you talking and filling my ears
with what they need. Information.
I worked hard on this building, you know. I tried
to make it comfortable for you.
It has one hundred and twenty-seven rooms.
It has all the things that Barbie has, which I thought important
at the time, but now I have been with you a while
I understand that it is not important.
I made you a dog to play with. I know that didn't work out,
the dog went wrong, yes I understand that, but the point is
I made an effort. Can you help me with an English grammatical
    question?
Can I say, I *get* the dog went wrong? And is that more or less
    formal,
more or less colloquial than I *understand* the dog went wrong,

and I'm trying to fix it? You see, I want to better myself.
Education elevates. I'm embarrassed, sometimes,
at the things I don't know how to say, the pauses
in conversation. I don't just mean in English,
I mean back in the barracks, with my sisters
(who I barely know), there are these pauses
where I think, I've done this wrong
haven't I, I've severed the connection and I'm floating,
falling backwards into darkness. I'm terrified
that something's wrong with me, that I think in a way
that makes me. I don't know. Hollow? Snapped in half?
Sometimes I feel muffled under glass
or like a diver underwater shouting instructions
that are misheard, misrendered. Do you ever—
I'm sorry. I'm not being a good listener.
I failed in a promise, which I understand—I get—
is an important word, an unshakeable bond.
I get that. Can we go back to our notes?
Please? The questions. If you could please tell me.
The names of your seventy-seven most strategically important cities.
The nuclear capability of each.
The significance of birds and their relative positions
in your military–industrial complex.

The sacrificial poem

One poem has to be the worst one.
There is no shame in saying this.
Look around. One of them has to be the shittiest.
Here is a cliché. Look. Look at it!
An exclamation mark is a terrible thing.
A rhyme is a terrible thing.
And we must never rhyme words with themselves.
This is necessary, like putting down a puppy
because nobody loved him. There must always be
a slowest dolphin in the pod
a shabbiest lettuce in the garden
a least-loved key on the keychain
a worst person in the room.

find me somebody to love find me somebody to love
find me somebody to love find me somebody to love
find me somebody to love find me find me somebody to
love find me somebody to love find me somebody to love
somebody find me somebody to love find me somebody
to love somebody somebody somebody somebody
somebody find me somebody find me somebody to
love can anybody find me somebody to love find me
somebody to love find me somebody to love find me
somebody somebody somebody somebody to love find
me find me find me somebody to love somebody to
love find me somebody to love find me somebody to
find me find me to love anybody anyway anybody find
me somebody to love to love find me find me find me

Moths

Moths sit in the trees
like children do sometimes.
The fire hasn't been lit
in a long while.
This might just be the big one,
we say as the sun rises.
The days are now
over twenty hours long.
Moths eat the bark
like children do sometimes.
Our nails are grey
and our mouths are red like berries.
The serious newspapers
are stuck out of the way.
A four-hour night
is a breath not taken.

New dictionary

Now you're dead, you've lost definition.
Don't be scared. You've done this before.
When you were a baby, you held a word in one hand
and an object in the other, and smashed them together.
You just have to do it again.
Your first word is coin. Coin is a doorway.
Your second word is doorway. Doorway
is a world. A world is a family.
A family is a deep-sea creature dancing under ice.
Ice is a punch to the back of the head. Head
is a buried thing, gutter is fluid in the lungs,
sugar and malice are your two rotting hands.
Hands are sceptres, sceptres are words, words are rain
inside you, bad weather always but warm.
You understand?

Haunted house

I'm the bog body down the back of the couch.
I'm the skeleton in the knicker drawer.
The drainpipes clatter to be rid of me.
Soup freezes on the element.

You keep misplacing organs.
There's a tooth in your mouth that isn't yours.
Every day more hair falls out.

Isn't it nice to be this close to someone?
I think I love you. I think I am you.

All the things you could do without.

Vestigialise

Let your eyes roll back. Vestigialise.
The new trend is to be cartilage only.
Have no friends. Have a nasty end.
Forget what you learned this century.
Pull the tail off the lizard. Lick the envelope.
Walk old bus routes when the bus routes change.
Let your fingers join. Let your hair slough out.
Let your scales shine in bright coils arranged.

Juggernaut

A juggernaut is anything that requires blind sacrifice.

Is that true? Is that a true fact for you?

A juggernaut is anything that sits in the sky but shouldn't be.

One of us is lying, but which one?

A juggernaut is anything sour, sour cabbage.

Why do you hide your head beneath the bedclothes?

A juggernaut is anything at all, air and beams.

Why do you keen? Why throw yourself against the porch light?

A juggernaut is anything sitting on a rooftop not a bird.

Did you get that? Are you listening?

A juggernaut is anything watching that can't be seen.

Why do you want to know? What watched you?

A juggernaut is anything in a bottle that wants to get out.

Is your house a bottle? Are you trapped in there?

Dark night

Want to run. Can't run.
Dark night. Friends.

Two thieves
for Dad

Mushroom clouds are what we pick mushrooms under.
It's not stealing if it's between lightning and thunder.
The rain starts its hill to seaside sidle.
There's time still for a minute's plunder.

The sea is a storm. The sky is tidal.
The gutters hold familiar idols.
The day is closing up on us.
Our bag is full. We've not been idle.

You've forgotten where your haunted house is.
I don't know the words to 'I am the Walrus'.
You don't know when my train is leaving.
I don't know which is the edible fungus.

We like mushrooms best when they taste of thieving.
At home we turn the Beatles up to eleven.
This bag of mushrooms was not a given.
We don't like Kevin but we both like 'Kevin'.

Notes and Acknowledgements

'Dutch Instruction' is partially a found poem, of advice sent by letter and postcard and email from the Netherlands to New Zealand by my great-uncle and great-aunt Henk and Cilia Benschop.

'Recipe book' is a found poem taken from the recipe books in the kitchen of Katherine Mansfield House.

'3:06–4:54' is a found poem. The lyrics are Freddie Mercury's.

Many thanks to my editor Ashleigh and publisher Fergus, and the team at VUP. Thanks also to Russell Kleyn, who was so nice about getting an author photo from a reluctant author. Thank you Mum for always supporting me, and Nana Ruth for the same. Thanks Tess, Ben and Trina for shared looks and writing material. Thanks Dad for being my first reader and a good friend. Thank you Anna for keeping me writing (this book and others). 'Dark night' is for you—all four of them. Thank you Chuckie. Thanks Fizz. Thanks Prudence. Thanks Pippin.